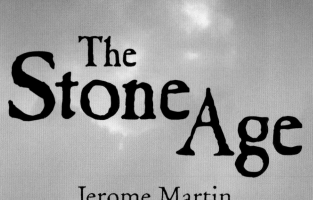

The
Stone Age

Jerome Martin

Illustrated by Colin King

Additional illustrations by Kimberley Scott

Designed by Amy Manning and Sam Whibley

Stone Age expert: Dr. Caroline McDonald, Museum of London
Reading consultant: Alison Kelly

Contents

Long, long ago

The Stone Age began a very, very long time ago, when the first people started making tools from stone.

It lasted until around 4,000 years ago.

Stone Age people also made tools from other natural things such as wood, bone, animal skins, deer antlers and plants.

On the move

For most of the Stone Age, people found food by gathering wild plants and hunting wild animals.

They lived in small groups. Each group moved from place to place to find enough food.

Sometimes dogs helped people to carry things.

People built simple shelters to sleep in.

They made fires for cooking food and keeping warm.

Tame dogs helped with hunting.

Stone tools

People made many different types of tools out of stone.

Hand axes were made for cutting meat or plants.

Arrows for hunting were made with stone tips.

Scrapers were used to clean animal skins for making clothes.

Good tool makers were very important people. They sat in the warmest spot near the fire.

Each stone tool had to be hammered and chipped into shape. It was very hard work.

First, a tool maker chose a stone of the right type, shape and size.

Next, she used an even harder stone to hammer off big pieces.

Finally, she used an antler to chip off small flakes and make a sharp edge.

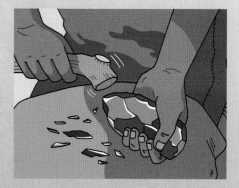

Hunting animals

People hunted wild animals for their meat.

Some hunters used fire to chase groups of bison until they fell over cliffs.

Other hunters trapped reindeer in narrow valleys. They threw spears at them.

People often used bows and arrows to shoot small animals and birds.

Some Stone Age hunters used arrows like these with stone points.

The points were attached to sticks using glue and string made from animal parts.

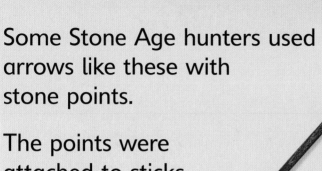

Feathers helped the arrows to fly straight.

In the Stone Age, both men and women went hunting.

Fishing

In the Stone Age, people had different ways of catching fish to eat.

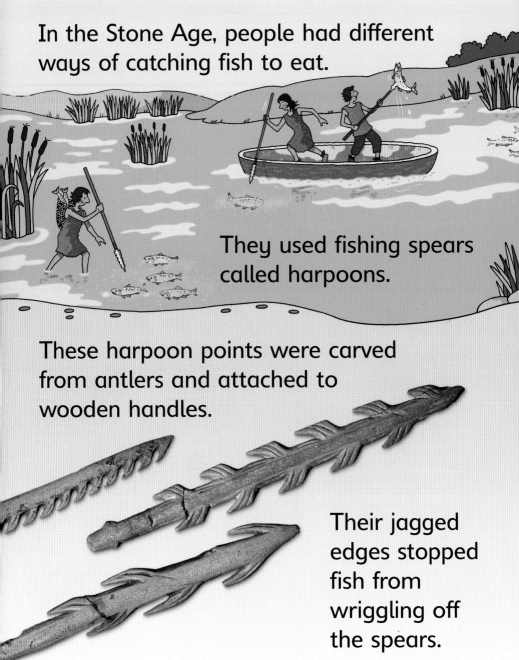

They used fishing spears called harpoons.

These harpoon points were carved from antlers and attached to wooden handles.

Their jagged edges stopped fish from wriggling off the spears.

They also used fish hooks made from bone, and fishing lines and nets made from twisted grass.

Stone Age people also invented clever traps for catching fish.

They blocked a fast-flowing stream with stones and a woven basket.

The water swept through holes in the basket while the fish got stuck inside.

Gathering food

Stone Age people didn't just hunt animals for food. They gathered wild food such as roots, berries, nuts and seeds.

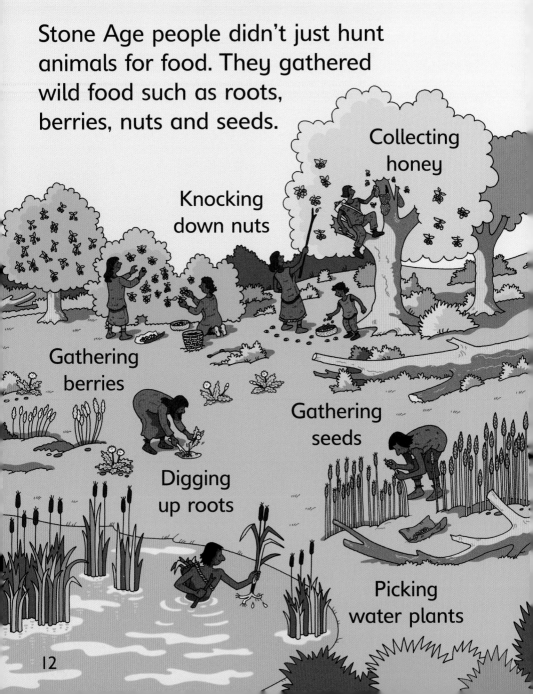

Collecting honey

Knocking down nuts

Gathering berries

Gathering seeds

Digging up roots

Picking water plants

They made a type of bread from the seeds of barley or wheat.

First, they used stones to crush the seeds into a powder.

Then they mixed the powder with water to make dough.

They baked the dough on flat rocks placed on a fire.

Grinding seeds took hours, and gave people very sore backs.

Oww!

Making clothes

Clothes were often made from the skins of animals such as deer.

People scraped the skins clean and then rubbed them until they were soft.

The skins were cut into pieces and holes were made in the edges with a stone tool.

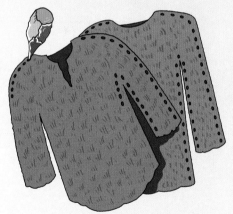

The pieces were stitched into warm clothes using needles made from bone.

People also wore
necklaces and bracelets like these.

They made the beads from shells, bones,
animal teeth and pebbles.

Sometimes sea shells were sewn
onto clothes for decoration.

15

Stone Age homes

People made different types of shelters, using whatever they could find nearby.

Huts were built using branches and lots of thick bundles of dry reeds.

Some people lived in caves. They blocked part of the entrance to keep out the wind.

Other people made homes from the bones and skins of huge animals called mammoths.

16

This is what a Stone Age hut might have looked like.

It is made from branches covered in soil and grass.

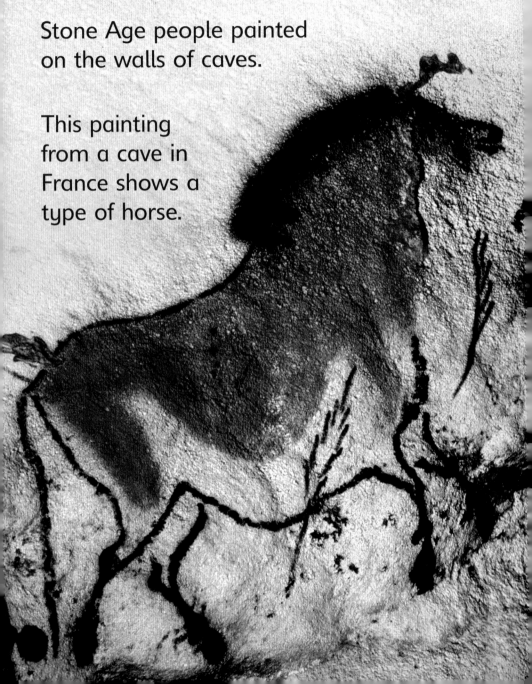

Cave painters

Stone Age people painted
on the walls of caves.

This painting
from a cave in
France shows a
type of horse.

For paint, people crushed up yellow or red rocks, or black soot from the fire.

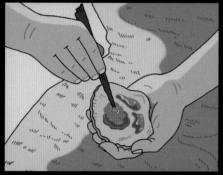

Then they mixed the powder with spit or with sticky animal fat.

They used their fingers, or brushes made of twigs, hair, moss or feathers.

Sometimes they made shapes by blowing paint over their hands.

Carving

Stone Age people also made elegant carvings from bones, antlers and tusks.

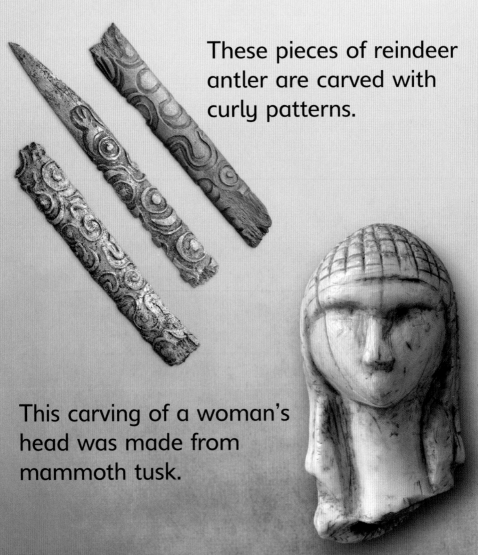

These pieces of reindeer antler are carved with curly patterns.

This carving of a woman's head was made from mammoth tusk.

Carving wasn't easy. It took lots of time.

First, the artist cut out a rough shape using a blade made from stone.

The shape was rubbed with fine sand and animal skin to smooth it.

A stone tool with a sharp point was used to carve fine lines and patterns.

People also carved flutes and whistles from hollow bird bones.

The first farmers

Some people discovered how to grow crops and raise animals for food. This is how the first farms started.

At first, people collected seeds from wild plants, and caught wild animals.

Then, they learned how to grow plants from the seeds and tame the animals.

Some farmers went to new places to find more land. Farming spread all over the world.

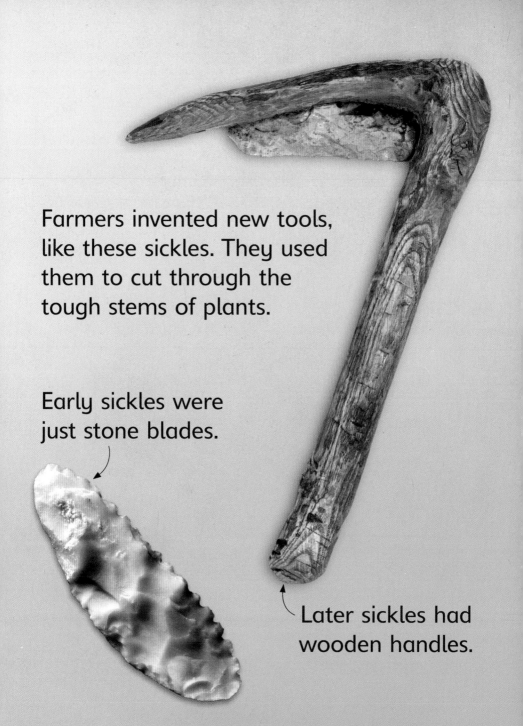

Farmers invented new tools, like these sickles. They used them to cut through the tough stems of plants.

Early sickles were just stone blades.

Later sickles had wooden handles.

Building houses

Now people were farming, they didn't need to keep moving around to find food. They stayed in one place.

They cut down trees to make fields and built big, strong houses to live in.

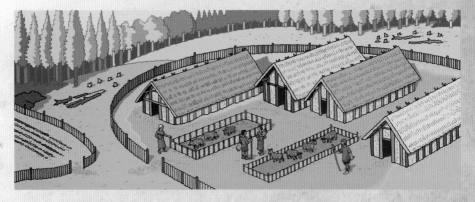

More and more people built fields and houses. These were the first villages.

People started making pots from baked clay. They used them for cooking and storing food.

These pots are from Sweden.

They are over 4,000 years old.

People often decorated pots by pressing shells or twisted rope into the wet clay.

Standing stones

At the end of the Stone Age, people built monuments using huge stones.

This famous monument is called Stonehenge. It's in England.

These huge stones were put up around 4,500 years ago.

Some of them have other stones lying on top of them.

The stones around the outside once formed a circle, but some of them have fallen over.

No one knows exactly what monuments like this were for.

How do we know?

Some Stone Age things have survived for thousands of years, buried in the ground or frozen in ice. Experts dig them up to find out more about life in the Stone Age.

This Stone Age home is 5,000 years old. It had a roof when people lived there.

Shelves

Entrance

Fireplace

Experts learn about Stone Age people by studying their bones and their tools.

Carvings and cave paintings teach them about early art, animals and hunting.

Some experts learn even more by living like Stone Age people.

Glossary

Here are some of the words in this book you might not know. This page tells you what they mean.

 antlers - bony spikes that grow from the heads of deer.

 bison - a large animal like a cow with a shaggy mane and a hump.

 harpoon - a spear with a jagged point, used for hunting fish.

 mammoth - an elephant-like animal with tusks that lived long ago.

 blade - a tool (or part of a tool) used for cutting.

 sickle - a curved tool with a sharp edge used for cutting plants.

 monument - a group of huge stones, often set up in a line or circle.

Websites to visit

You can visit exciting websites to find out more about the Stone Age. For links to sites with video clips and activities, go to the Usborne Quicklinks website at **www.usborne.com/quicklinks** and type in the keywords **"beginners stone age"**.

Always ask an adult before using the internet and make sure you follow these basic rules:

1. Never give out personal information, such as your name, address, school or telephone number.

2. If a website asks you to type in your name or email address, check with an adult first.

The websites are regularly reviewed and the links at Usborne Quicklinks are updated. However, Usborne Publishing is not responsible and does not accept liability for the content or availability of any website other than its own. We recommend that children are supervised while on the internet.

This bison is carved from a reindeer antler. It's around 15,000 years old.

Index

Acknowledgments

Photographic manipulation by John Russell
Picture research by Ruth King

Photo credits

The publishers are grateful to the following for permission to reproduce material:
Cover © Jean-Daniel Sudres/Hemis/Corbis; **p1** © Martin Zwick/age fotostock/Superstock; **p6**
(top) © The Trustees of the British Museum; **(middle)** © De Agostini/N. Cirani/Getty Images; **(bottom)**
© The Trustees of the Natural History Museum, London; **p9** © DTaggart84319/iStock; **p10** © RMN-Grand
Palais (musée d'Archéologie nationale)/Jean Schormans; **p15** © RMN-Grand Palais (musée d'Archéologie
nationale)/Jean Schormans; **p17** © Peter Howard; **p18** © Glasshouse Images/Alamy; **p20 (top)** ©
RMN-Grand Palais (musée d'Archéologie nationale)/Loïc Hamon; **(bottom)** © RMN-Grand Palais (musée
d'Archéologie nationale)/Jean-Gilles Berizzi; **p23 (top)** © Museum of London; **(bottom)** © Album/ASF/
Album alb2106827/Superstock; **p25** © DEA/G. Dagli Orti/Getty Images; **p26-27** © Jason Hawkes/Getty
Images; **p28-29** © Worldwide Picture Library/Alamy; **p31** © Hervé Champollion/akg-images.

First published in 2015 by Usborne Publishing Ltd., Usborne House, 83-85 Saffron Hill, London EC1N
8RT, England. www.usborne.com Copyright © 2015 Usborne Publishing Ltd. The name Usborne and the
devices ♀ ♥ are Trade Marks of Usborne Publishing Ltd.

Sun, moon and stars

Farm animals

Elizabeth I

Rubbish & Recycling

Dogs

Horses and ponies

Spiders

Planes

Cats

Ancient Greeks

VOLCANOES

DINOSAURS

Your Body

Armour

Sharks

Celts

VIKINGS

Castles

How flowers grow

Digging up the past

Living in space

Caterpillars and Butterflies

Ballet

Pirates

EGYPTIANS

Eggs and Chicks

ROMANS

Weather

Tadpoles and frogs

Why do we eat?

Under the sea

Bears

AZTECS

TRUCKS

Night Animals

Firefighters

Antarctica

Bugs

COWBOYS

Planet Earth

London

Seashore

China

Dangerous Animals

Rainforests

Trees

Reptiles

Ships

Bats

Penguins